Introduction

Why choose a guinea-pig? Dogs need to be exercised regularly and cats, although they do not need walks, may sharpen their claws on the upholstery. Budgerigars and canaries cannot be handled easily and are not 'cuddly' animals; the same applies to tortoises and fish. Golden and dwarf hamsters are nocturnal, becoming active at dusk, and so are less suitable for children. Also, if they are handled a little roughly at times, they tend to give their owner quite a nip. Finally, they will live for only 2–3 years at the most.

The fact that guinea-pigs can easily be left on their own in the house – occasionally for a whole day, provided they have suitably prepared food – is a definite advantage. Further plusses are that they are active by day and will allow themselves to be stroked and cuddled. Guinea-pigs are ideal pets, particularly for children aged from about 5 years upwards. For adults who may never have kept a pet before, a guinea-pig can also be an ideal first-time pet for a variety of reasons.

Those of you who have had the opportunity to get to know guinea-pigs more closely will probably never want to be without these lovable domestic pets again. The same goes for the old, or people with some physical disability, particularly if they live in a place where keeping dogs or cats is a problem. Guinea-pigs can reach an age of 5–8 years, sometimes even longer if they are kept properly. They have an inborn reluctance to bite other animals, or human beings, and will bite or scratch much less frequently than other domestic pets, such as rabbits.

3

Things to consider beforehand

As with all domestic pets, acquiring and keeping a guinea-pig involves taking responsibility for a living creature and engaging in a regular daily routine of care, feeding and cleaning. If only one animal is kept it will also need a certain amount of contact with its owner.

If you acquire a young animal, you will have to look after it constantly throughout its lifetime. As a rule, however, a guinea-pig will not mind very much if you hand it over to friends, a pet holiday-home or possibly a specialist pet-store to be looked after during your holidays.

Equipping a cage

For one or several guinea-pigs, you will need a cage with a floor area of at least 80 × 60 cm (32 × 24 in), preferably consisting of a plastic tray with an easily removable, barred upper portion. It should be 35–50 cm (14–20 in) high to allow the inmates to stand upright should they wish. The cage should be light and must never be positioned in a draught.

Your guinea-pigs will enjoy being allowed to run about in the house, or even in the garden, if the weather permits, but this is not an essential part of keeping the animal properly.

Guinea-pigs are herbivores and will be quite content with hay, vegetables, fruit, greenfood, oats and the usual ready-prepared food available from pet-stores.

They use hay not just for food but also for soft bedding, and sawdust or wood shavings will serve as an absorbent layer on the floor of the cage. All are readily available from pet-stores and some supermarkets.

A food-dish, preferably made of glazed pottery, a hay-rack, a water-bottle and perhaps a sleeping-box will complete the furnishings.

Choosing a guinea-pig

One guinea-pig or a pair?
If you intend to keep just one guinea-pig, the sex of the animal will not play an important role in your choice. If you are thinking of keeping two or more guinea-pigs, however, experience has shown that female guinea-pigs always get on well with each other. This also applies if further females are added to the group later on.

Previous pages: Guinea-pigs make very delight-ful pets.

Opposite: This white Abyssinian guinea-pig is peering out of its basket with a highly alert and interested expression.

A wide range of func-tional cages for guinea-pigs can be found in pet-stores.

5

Opposite: *The shiny, slightly moist-looking eyes are characteristic of a healthy guinea-pig.*

The situation with male guinea-pigs is rather different. Even if they have no visual or scent contact with females of their species, males, as adults, may often be aggressive towards each other. This occasionally leads to injuries, particularly if another guinea-pig is introduced to the quarters of one which has already been living on its own.

If you decide to keep a pair of guinea-pigs, remember that they have a habit of multiplying 'like rabbits' so that you will soon have a vast number of them. Also remember that only young animals can be passed on through pet-stores. Invariably, whenever you have a surplus, you will find that the pet-store is not interested in acquiring any young animals!

A young guinea-pig or an older one?

If you decide to buy a guinea-pig from a pet-store, you should always choose a young animal. It will find it easier to get used to human beings and its age is easier to estimate.

Of course, even fully grown guinea-pigs can become completely tame, although it may take a little longer under certain circumstances. On the other hand, from a welfare angle, you would be doing a good deed if you decided to take on a fully grown animal from an animal-care home. As a rule, it is impossible to assess the age of fully grown guinea-pigs accurately.

In general, guinea-pigs can attain an age of 5–8 years, rarely live beyond 10 years.

How to recognize a healthy guinea-pig

Do not allow yourself to be influenced by the retailer and once you have decided on a particular guinea-pig, watch it for a while. A healthy animal will run around actively in its cage and sit normally without being hunched up or arching its back.

Take a look around its cage and see whether the droppings are of the normal, fairly long 'bean' shape or whether there is any indication at all of **diarrhoea**. If there is any suspicion of diarrhoea, even if the animal you have chosen does not display sticky faeces or dirt around its anus, you should think twice about purchasing it and either go elsewhere or, at least, postpone your purchase for a few days.

Do not even consider buying an animal with scruffy or **dull-looking fur, scaly patches** or **scurf** visible beneath healthy-looking fur, or bare patches on any part of its body. More or less circular hairless patches indicate fungal infection, or the presence of mites, which can be spread easily from one guinea-pig to another.

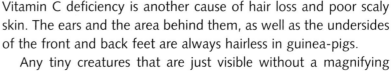

Vitamin C deficiency is another cause of hair loss and poor scaly skin. The ears and the area behind them, as well as the undersides of the front and back feet are always hairless in guinea-pigs.

Any tiny creatures that are just visible without a magnifying glass are are usually **lice**. You will find their whitish yellow eggs sticking to the individual hairs of their host. Lice are not dangerous in small numbers but it is not advisable to purchase animals infested in this way.

You should definitely insist on being allowed to touch and pick up the guinea-pig. Animals are generally not cared for individually by pet-store-keepers so you should not be put off by any apparent shyness on the part of the guinea-pig. Only by holding an animal in your hand will you be able to tell what kind of condition it is in with respect to nourishment. If it is **very thin** and you can count the individual ribs or vertebrae, you should not buy it.

Even an expert will often find it difficult to distinguish whether an animal's condition is due to inadequate feeding, with food of insufficient quality, or to a disease. In the case of mature males in particular check that the **anal area** is not distended by droppings.

You should not buy a guinea-pig that is **fat**. As a rule, this is almost never a problem with young animals, or even half-grown or recently fully grown individuals, but if an animal seems to be overweight you can reckon on the possibility of heart or liver damage later on.

A healthy guinea-pig will have shiny, slightly moist **eyes**. Runny eyes indicate serious health problems.

A healthy guinea-pig should never have any **crusty deposits** around the eyes or nostrils. You should check the area around the eyes thoroughly for any signs of crustiness or scaliness.

Next, carefully examine its **mouth**. If you are right-handed, support the neck of the upright guinea-pig with your right hand so that you can open its mouth with your thumb and index finger. Use your left hand to support the pelvis and thighs of the animal while performing this procedure.

Check that the two **incisor teeth** and the **molars** of the upper jaw just touch those of the lower jaw. This indicates that the teeth are in order and are being worn down properly.

This is very important. If the incisors are not being worn down properly they will grow too long and the animal will find feeding difficult. This occurs particularly when the incisors of the upper and

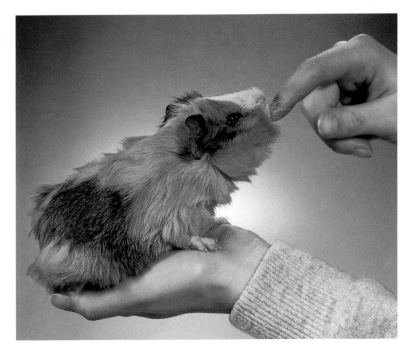

Careful and regular observation by the owner is the best prerequisite for a healthy guinea-pig.

lower jaws do not touch each other and so tend to grow past each other.

In extreme cases, when the animal's ability to take nourishment is affected, it will start to lose weight. You should not acquire any guinea-pig whose teeth have not developed properly because, unless you are willing to trim back the teeth regularly yourself, constant correction by a veterinarian will be necessary.

Finally, take a good look at the naked pads of the **front and hind feet** for any signs of inflammation, scurf or abscesses. The latter will generally heal badly. These problems, along with claws that are overlong or grow in all directions, are usually found in older animals.

If you consider all these points before purchasing a guinea-pig, you can be reasonably sure that you are dealing with a really healthy animal. Provided that you continue to check these health points while the guinea-pig is in your care, you will usually be able to identify any illnesses at an early stage, when help and treatment by a veterinarian are still possible.

Adjustment period

Once you have brought your new pet home safely, it should be put in its prepared cage right away and left to its own devices for a while. At first, the guinea-pig will probably crawl into a corner, where it will hide under some hay. This is quite normal behaviour in new, unfamiliar surroundings. Later on, when it feels that no-one is watching, it will begin to explore its new home. Even then, although it may seem hard to wait, you should not attempt to take it out of its cage and allow it to run around because it might easily escape. Guinea-pigs are naturally shy animals and quickly become restless and excited.

This will all change later on. A guinea-pig will, for example, stand upright against the wall of the cage when it hears its owner's voice. It will also learn to distinguish quite clearly between those who regularly give it food and everyone else. This is demonstrated by the fact that it will start to squeak – meaning 'I'm hungry!' – whenever its usual carer approaches.

Most guinea-pigs love to be able to retreat into the shelter of a cosy box, like the one shown in the illustration. A box like this should have a floor area of about 15 × 25 cm (6 × 10 in) and a height of about 15 cm (6 in). There should be a hole large enough for the guinea-pig to pass through comfortably. This little 'house' has no separate floor and so will stay clean for some time. Guinea-pigs are particularly fond of resting on the roof of these houses.

A shelter like this should not be placed in the cage until the guinea-pig has settled into its new home. A very shy animal will tend to stay inside it for a long time, unless it feels really undisturbed and unobserved.

During the early days in particular, beware of frightening the animal with loud noises. It is a good idea to make a constant, quiet, calm, buzzing noise when approaching the cage, particularly during the period of adjustment. The guinea-pig will learn to distinguish between its owner's voice and those of others within a few short weeks.

The right kind of accommodation for your guinea-pigs

A cage indoors
As mentioned on page 5, guinea-pigs which are housed indoors are nowadays usually kept in cages consisting of a firm plastic **tray** and a barred **upper section** that can be easily snapped on or off and removed. These can be obtained from pet-stores.

If the **walls** of the tray are too low, the area around the cage will soon become littered with the bedding and dirt which falls out of the cage. On the other hand, if they are too high, the guinea-pigs will be prevented from looking out and having constant contact with the rest of their surroundings. **Box-type containers** with a ventilated hood, incorporating a transparent plastic strip as well as **vivariums**, are other options but they do tend to cut off the guinea-pigs from their surroundings. In addition, it is difficult to ventilate these types of container adequately.

Guinea-pigs may also be kept in a **wooden box** that is open at the top or covered with a mesh lid, although this is not recommended. Note that guinea-pigs are quite unable to jump out of a container that is taller than about 50 cm (20 in).

The guinea-pigs' home should always be placed in a **draught-free** position with natural **daylight**.

Guinea-pigs are happy to be able to run around in the house but they should only be allowed out under constant supervision because carpets, furniture and especially electrical flexes may be gnawed. Unlike rabbits, guinea-pigs can never be house-trained and they will deposit urine and faeces anywhere. Also, they will not come out from beneath items of furniture or from hiding places when you call them.

This cage is sufficiently spacious for two or three guinea-pigs and it can be opened from the top. It has a floor area of at least 80 × 60 cm (32 × 24 in) and is 35–50 cm (14–20 in) high.

Use **sawdust** or **wood shavings** as litter in the cage. Dry peat

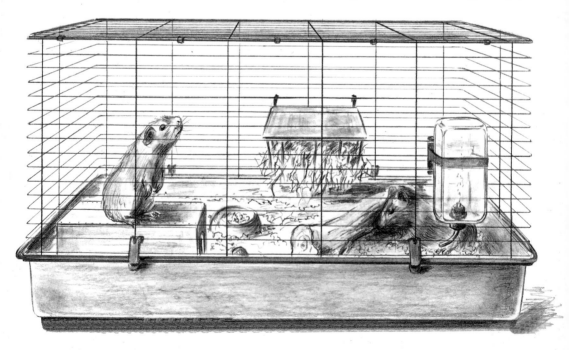

moss, which creates dust and may cause respiratory diseases, is quite unsuitable. Moist peat moss is even more harmful because guinea-pigs cannot stand dampness. The litter should be changed regularly at least twice a week. It is a good idea to put a layer of newspaper beneath the wood shavings to facilitate cleaning out.

Put a layer of good-quality **hay** on top of the wood shavings. The hay will also be eaten by the guinea-pigs. To prevent soiling of the hay, which is such an important part of a good diet, fix up a **hay-rack**. This rack should be closed over with a sturdy, slanting lid because guinea-pigs love to observe their surroundings from a lofty vantage point.

Ideally, guinea-pigs that live indoors should be kept at a **temperature** somewhere between 18 and 22°C (64 and 72°F) and at a relative **humidity** of between 40 and 70 per cent. Avoid rapid temperature fluctuations because these are likely to be harmful. The air in the vicinity of a radiator will often become too dry and can make these rodents prone to diseases of the respiratory tract.

A hutch and/or run in the garden

While guinea-pigs can be kept as domestic pets in the home, especially where space outdoors is not available, they can equally well be housed outdoors in a **hutch** in the garden. This may be advisable if you want to keep them on a larger scale, e.g., in order to breed different colour varieties or fur types.

Outdoor hutches of the type used for rabbits are equally suitable for guinea-pigs. With sufficient warm, dry bedding, in the form of hay, and with part of the front enclosed, guinea-pigs can usually survive most winters, provided that the temperature does not fall below −10°C (14°F) for long periods of time. Of course, animals that are to be kept outside in the winter should be allowed to get used to outside conditions during the warmer part of the

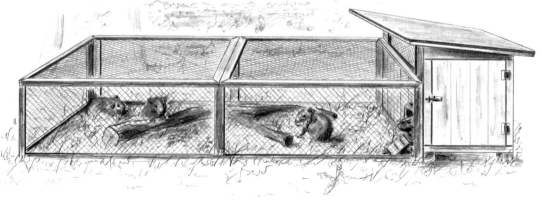

14

year so that they can adjust to seasonally fluctuating temperatures. Never transfer a guinea-pig from the warmth of a pet-store to an outside hutch during the winter months.

A removable, length of wood should be placed behind the mesh-covered door of these guinea-pig hutches, to prevent not only the animals but also the bedding from falling out when the door is opened.

The width of the **bars** or gauge of the **wire-mesh** should be small enough to prevent mice from entering the hutch. The planed planks of wood from which the hutch is built should be of the **tongued-and-grooved** type to prevent draughts. The outside of the roof should be covered with roofing felt to protect the guinea-pigs' home from rainwater. Damp conditions in the hutch are likely to prove fatal .

Whether it is sited on a balcony or in a garden, this type of accommodation should have stout legs so that dampness from the ground cannot penetrate from beneath.

Accommodation like this can be equipped with a **fenced run**. It is more practical to make the run portable so that it can be moved

about on a lawn to allow the guinea-pigs to graze. The run must be enclosed on all sides, even from above, to keep away cats and birds of prey. The wire should have a small-gauge mesh as a cat may cleverly insert a paw through wide-mesh wire and try to attack a guinea-pig. As a guide, 2.5 × 1.25 cm (1 × 1 1/2 in) mesh should be adequate.

Guinea-pigs should only be allowed out in their run during periods of warm, dry weather because they are quite sensitive to cold, damp ground. On the other hand, they can quickly become overheated and may succumb to heat stroke as a result.

Example of an outside hutch designed for four groups of guinea-pigs. The roof, side walls and back wall are covered with roofing felt on the outside. Do not allow the guinea-pigs to nibble this though, because it is likely to be harmful.

Whenever they are allowed to run about outside, a portion of the run should therefore always be in shade and adequate drinking water must always be available.

During the night, 'garden guinea-pigs' should always be locked up in their hutch, or house, in case the temperature drops suddenly or it begins to rain. At this time, they are also more vulnerable to predators, e.g. foxes, which may scare them badly, even if they cannot be reached directly.

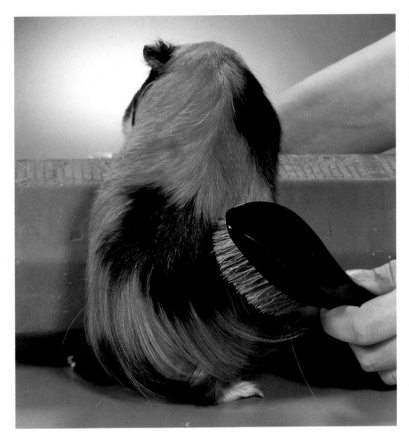

Caring for your guinea-pigs

Caring for guinea-pigs is particularly easy. Smooth-haired and Abyssinian guinea-pigs should not need brushing or combing at all if they are kept under normal conditions. The animals should be groomed only in exceptional circumstances, e.g. before a show, using a brush with soft bristles. In the case of Peruvian or other long-haired guinea-pigs, the fur towards the rear of the body in particular will require **daily combing** to prevent it from becoming tangled and matted. This is often caused by bits of hay or even wood shavings and, once the hair has become matted, the only solution is to cut it out. Obviously you should try to avoid this state of affairs being reached but, if necessary, the felty tangle should be carefully lifted away from the skin before it is cut.

Guinea-pigs are easy to care for.

Guinea-pigs do not need to be **bathed** and do not like it. If they do get very dirty and bathing becomes necessary, you should use only the mildest type of baby shampoo and be sure to rinse it off well. Afterwards, the fur must be dried thoroughly, perhaps gently

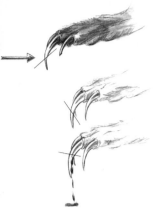

with a hairdryer, and the guinea-pig must be kept in warm surroundings, since these animals easily catch a chill.

Older guinea-pigs often experience problems with their **claws**, which they are unable to wear down properly. It is not unusual for the claws to grow irregularly or to become bent or wavy, or even corkscrew-like. It is important to cut them regularly, so that the animal can continue to walk properly.

This is a relatively simple task if the claws are not heavily pigmented, because the upper part, which is visibly filled with blood vessels, can easily be distinguished from the 'dead' part. Cut off a few millimetres of the excess with special nail-clippers, so that the end of the claw is slightly slanted downwards. Dark-coloured claws are more difficult to cut because the part containing the blood vessels is much harder to distinguish.

How you cut is important! Correct (top). The cut should be made following the profile of the claw. Wrong: Cutting against the line of growth or cutting too high up.

To be on the safe side, do not cut off too much of the claw. If there is any bleeding, press a small ball of cottonwool, soaked in an alum solution, onto the affected part for a few moments. Pressure alone will often stop the bleeding very quickly. Such problems with claws can also be dealt with by a veterinarian.

Guinea-pigs possess a perineal 'pocket' near the anus, in which faeces often accumulate. This occurs particularly in older males. By exerting slight pressure from the outside inwards (best from both sides), you can help rid your guinea-pig of this regularly accumulating collection of faeces. This task will need to be carried out each day. Plenty of roughage in the diet may help to alleviate the problem but essentially it is a sign of old age, for which there is no cure. The cause is a loss of muscle tone.

How to hold a guinea-pig when cutting its claws.

The finest hay fibres or even hairs may become caught under the foreskin of young male guinea-pigs. This is because the tip of the penis has a tiny barb on each side. These fine hairs and bits of fibre can also penetrate the lower part of the urethra. In such cases, they should be carefully removed. Look out for this problem when you handle your pet.

Opposite: Satisfaction all round: this guinea-pig is healthy and is feeling good.

Opposite: *Guinea-pigs live primarily on hay and greenfood. Lettuces, green cabbage, carrots and also cucumbers and apples are very sought after.*

The right foods for your guinea-pigs

In the wild, the staple diet of guinea-pigs is mainly **grasses** and other **plant matter**, both of which are rich in raw fibres and relatively poor in nutrients. This is why a guinea-pig has such an extremely long intestine compared with the size of its body. If you want your pets to stay healthy for a long time and to have an attractive, shiny coat, a diet rich in raw fibres is essential.

This type of food is bitten off or gnawed with the help of the incisors, or gnawing teeth, and then chewed up thoroughly by the molars, while being lubricated well with saliva. This is all part of the digestive process because the saliva, which is produced by the salivary glands, contains important digestive enzymes. In addition, this type of diet means that guinea-pigs need to eat relatively small amounts of food at fairly frequent intervals.

There is another special feature of guinea-pig nourishment that is important to remember. Guinea-pigs, like marmosets, the

great apes and human beings, are among the few mammals which are unable to produce **Vitamin C** (ascorbic acid) in their bodies. Therefore they have to obtain their entire requirement of Vitamin C from the food that they eat. Under normal conditions, guinea-pigs require a daily dose of 16 mg Vitamin C per kilogram of body weight but, under conditions of stress, when there is risk of infection, or during pregnancy, they may even require as much as 30 mg/kg. This means you should check the Vitamin C content of the different foodstuffs that you give your guinea-pig.

For example, you should never give rabbit food to guinea-pigs, especially on a regular basis, because it is unlikely to contain sufficient of this vital vitamin. Also, you should not exceed the recommended use-by-date on guinea-pig food because its Vitamin C will decline accordingly. For the same reason, the food should be kept in a sealed container.

A pottery food-dish, with two compartments and rounded-off inner surfaces, which cannot be tipped over easily.

You should also make sure that the hay offered is of absolutely top quality. It should never be dusty, damp, musty, mouldy or spoiled in any way. Also note that freshly mown hay can cause health problems. Hay needs to be well ventilated for at least 6 weeks after harvesting.

Above and opposite:
Offer your guinea-pigs high-energy food – but only in small amounts. Carrots are still preferred, as can be seen here.

Greenfood and hay is a good mixture for the spring.

Hay and greenfoods

During the summer months, in addition to a wide variety of **grasses**, offer your guinea-pigs plenty of greenfood, especially dandelions (*Taraxacum* spp.), along with their flowers, and also **plants** such as yarrow (*Achillea* spp.), greater plantain (*Plantago major*), ribwort plantain (*Plantago lanceolata*), hogweed (*Heracleum sphondylium*), chickweed (*Stellaria media*), lucerne (*Medicago sativa*) and red and white clover (*Trifolium* spp.). Some plants, e.g. bracken (*Pteridium aquilinum*) and ragwort (*Senecio* spp.), should never be given. Greenfood should only ever be cut from areas that are free from contamination with dog mess and harmful substances, e.g. pesticides, traffic pollution. Any dust should be washed off but greenfood wet from rain or dew is not harmful.

In the spring, very young plants (particularly lucerne and red and white clover), although very rich in protein, are poor in raw fibres and so should be given in only small amounts. This is best done by mixing the greenfood well with hay. The guinea-pigs will still try to pluck out just the leaf-blades, stalks and tiny leaves of the greenfood but it means that they will eat the greenfood much more slowly than if it were 'neat', i.e. unmixed with hay.

At times when there is not enough greenfood available, you

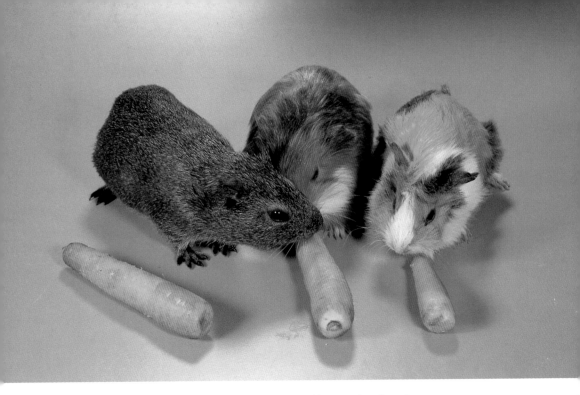

should give your guinea-pigs a variety of different kinds of **vegetables** and **fruits** in order to ensure an adequate supply of Vitamin C in their diet.

All types of lettuce may be offered – round lettuce, everlasting lettuce, endive, etc. – as well as chicory, Chinese leaves, lamb's lettuce and parsley. Green cabbage is the best type of cabbage to give them. It is the variety least likely to cause flatulence and contains large amounts of Vitamin C, as does broccoli.

Savoy cabbage, cauliflower (the white 'flowers' as well as the leaves) and kohl-rabi (including the leaves) can also be offered, but only in very small amounts because they incur an increased risk of bloating and indigestion. This is even more of a problem with white cabbage. For the same reason, red cabbage should not be given to guinea-pigs at all.

Carrots are a naturally valuable food item for guinea-pigs because they contain large amounts of carotene (the precursor of Vitamin A). Vitamin A in particular is absolutely essential for growth, maintaining the condition of the skin and mucous membranes, the functioning of the eyes, and many metabolic processes.

Apples are also an outstanding dietary item, especially when fresh. Windfalls are ideal from late summer to autumn, and are

Vitamins, especially Vitamin C, are absolutely indispensable.

23

sold cheaply by many orchards. They are full of vitamins and do not contain a great deal of sugar. Cut out any damaged areas and wash the apples before giving them to your guinea-pigs. It can help to slice the fruit into small pieces for them.

Pears should only be given in small amounts, as a titbit, because they contain large quantities of highly digestible sugars that can easily lead to bloating and fermentation processes. As a rule, give only ripe apples or pears.

Guinea-pigs are passionately fond of **cucumbers** and **melons**. Cucumbers are relatively poor in nutrients and are therefore a particularly good food item for well-nourished or slightly over-weight guinea-pigs.

Ready-prepared foods

Oats or oatflakes can be offered as **high-energy** or **concentrated** food, whereas many of the ready-prepared foods offered in pet-stores, such as maize or shredded maize, are far too rich in nutrients. These concentrated foods are especially valuable for guinea-pigs living outdoors during cold weather, because they provide an excellent source of energy. Make sure that only 10–20 g (about ¹/₂ oz) daily per kilogram of the guinea-pig's body weight are given from this range of concentrated foods.

If you are in the habit of feeding your guinea-pigs with old, dry bread (particularly white bread), crispbread or crackers, remember that these are all forms of concentrated, high-energy foods, and should be allowed for when calculating the daily ration.

You should never give a guinea-pig **cereal-type** or **pelleted**

A water-bottle can be fixed to the cage from the outside and is easy to clean and refill.

Bread is a high-energy food and should only be given in limited quantities.

food as the sole item in its diet. In addition, your pet should receive a total of 40–70 g (1^1/$_2$–2^1/$_2$ oz) of various juicy foods, together with unrestricted amounts of hay. This is the best way to ensure that your guinea-pig remains healthy.

Drinking water

Fresh drinking water must be supplied daily. The ideal way is in a **water-bottle** and this should be thoroughly cleaned on a regular

Drinking water should stand for a while before being offered to guinea-pigs but it should still be renewed every day. A water-bottle is a better container than a dish, which can become soiled very easily.

basis with a bottle-brush. The bottle is easily clipped onto the wire mesh of the cage, hutch or run.

It is a simple matter to enrich the water with Vitamin C if necessary. Solutions of Vitamin C can be obtained from a veterinarian or a pharmacy. Add approximately 20–40 mg of the vitamin to 100 ml (3½ fl. oz) water. If in doubt about using this sort of product, ask your veterinarian for advice.

Colour varieties and fur types of guinea-pigs

Compared with its ancestor, a subspecies of the wild guinea-pig (*Cavia aperea tschudii*) that inhabits the High Andes range, domestic guinea-pigs are larger, more massive, more compact and, one might even say, more plumply built.

Colour varieties

A wide range of colour varieties can be found in the domestic guinea-pig.

First of all, there is the normal, **agouti** colour, as seen in the wild species. This is a non-uniform colour, comparable to that of wild rabbits. This term is borrowed from the South American rodent, the agouti. When this colour has a sheen of gold to it, we speak of **golden agouti** guinea-pigs. If the brown tone of the original wild colour is missing – due to a mutation – we speak of **silver agouti**, a colour similar to that of the chinchilla.

You will also encounter **self**-coloured guinea-pigs ranging from **red** through shades of **gold** to **beige** and **saffron**. There are also **black** guinea-pigs, as well as the hitherto fairly rare **blues** – actually, rather more blue-grey – a shade resembling that found in 'blue' cats, and something like that of blue Viennese rabbits. You may also find **chocolate-brown** and **lilac** guinea-pigs.

Albino guinea-pigs are pure white. This means that the skin and fur, and the iris of the eyes, contain no pigmentation, so they are colourless. Because the irises lack any pigment, the blood vessels at the back of the eyes show through and the eye appears to be red.

Himalayan guinea-pigs are animals with white bodies and extremities. They are pure white at birth but, later, the so-called 'points' of the body darken, i.e. the area above the nose and the ears and the paws turn blackish to black-brown, or sometimes lighter. In these guinea-pigs, the eyes always lack pigmentation so they appear red.

Naturally, as with other domestic pets, there are guinea-pigs with partial loss of pigmentation, which means that they have a patched appearance. The fur of these animals may be two colours and, as a rule, is white with patches of red, yellow, black, etc. Animals with patches are a special case and are referred to as **tortoiseshell.** Where there is also white on the coat they are called **tortoiseshell and white**, or 'tortie and white' for short. If the black and red hairs merge they are known as **grindles.**

There are even wild-coloured guinea-pigs with patches of yellow or red, as well as with a very specific, irregular alternation of black with white. Numerous mutations and variations of colour and patching also occur. One of the more recent is the **Dalmatian,** which, like the Dalmatian dog, is spotted but with a dark head and a white blaze.

Top left: *Tri-coloured Abyssinian guinea-pig.*
Top right: *White Abyssinian guinea-pig.*
Bottom left: *Tri-coloured guinea-pig with fur that is long mainly on its back.*
Bottom right: *An agouti (wild-coloured) smooth-haired guinea-pig that is very similar to a wild guinea-pig in appearance.*

These long-haired guinea-pigs are pets rather than exhibition stock. Top left: Red and white guinea-pig. Top right: Tortoiseshell guinea-pig. Bottom left: A white-patched agouti guinea-pig. Bottom right: Agouti (wild-coloured) guinea-pig.

Fur types

The different colours mentioned above occur naturally in guinea-pigs of every fur type.

Normal or **smooth-haired** guinea-pigs are animals whose fur length and structure resembles that of the wild forms. A shiny satin variant has now become established and is becoming increasingly popular.

The rosette or **Abyssinian** guinea-pigs have longer and sometimes coarser fur than normal. In these guinea-pigs, the entire body is usually covered with rosettes. Raised ridges of fur are present where the rosettes meet and nowhere should the coat lie flat. The pattern of rosettes is very important for show purposes. As a rule, the rosettes are arranged symmetrically on each side of the body. There are, however, some specimens which lack individual rosettes on some parts of the body. If a rosette is missing halfway down the back, the guinea-pig may look as if it is wearing a saddle.

A speciality breed has been created in which the animals have fur that is normal except for a single rosette on the forehead. This is known as the **crested** guinea-pig. In the case of the **American crested** the colour of the crest differs from that of the coat, e.g. the guinea-pig may be red with a white crest. In the **English crested** guinea-pig the colour of the crest is the same as that of the body.

The original form of the long-haired guinea-pig is known as the **Peruvian.** The distinguishing feature of this variety is that long fur occurs on the head as well as the body. The length of the body fur may exceed 30 cm (12 in). In the case of the **sheltie**, however, the fur on the head is of normal length, while the longer body fur trails down each side of the body.

There is another variety of long-haired guinea-pig called the **coronet.** In these animals the fur on the rear of the guinea-pigs's body is elongated, forming a kind of train. The head has short hair and a crest on top.

Long-haired guinea-pigs require careful daily combing.

One of the most popular of the guinea-pig fur types is the **rex**, better known in North America as the **teddy**, because of the woolly appearance which is especially evident in older animals. Young rex guinea-pigs have coats which are wavier than old ones. There is a long-haired version of the rex guinea-pig, called the **Texel.**

Guinea-pig shows take place regularly in many different countries, with the entries being judged according to the standards laid down for each variety. You should be able to track down the address of a guinea-pig club from your local library or from specialist magazines. Contacting breeders is also another good way of obtaining more unusual varieties of guinea-pigs and show-quality stock.

How to handle your guinea-pigs

Guinea-pigs are relatively shy creatures. If they are not used to the experience, they do not like to allow themselves to be caught. If you try to catch them from above, they will instinctively try to escape. This reaction is inherited from their forebears, which, in the wild, often fall victim to predators.

The best way to hold a guinea-pig is by grasping it behind the front legs, enclosing its back with the thumb and fingers so that

the back is covered by the inside of your hand. The other hand can then be used to support the guinea-pig beneath its chest and stomach. For extra security, small children should carefully and gently press the guinea-pig against their chest to avoid dropping it.

What to do if a guinea-pig escapes

A guinea-pig can be surprisingly agile and, if it is allowed to roam freely around a room, it will often very quickly disappear under the furniture. If it is out of reach, you may have to wait patiently for a long time until it emerges again. It is possible to catch a guinea-pig with a net but the animal will soon learn what the net is for and will be even more careful to avoid capture in future.

Carefully grasp the guinea-pig and lift it up, providing it with adequate support so that it will not struggle or become upset.

You should never allow even the tamest guinea-pig to roam freely outside in the garden, but should keep it in a properly fenced-off run. Guinea-pigs can disappear like lightning into bushes or high grass and, even if they have strikingly coloured fur, they will be very difficult to find and catch again. They will usually fall prey to cats, dogs or foxes soon after making their escape.

Transporting your guinea-pigs

At some point, when you are travelling or on holiday, you will have to decide whether to take your guinea-pigs with you or leave them behind in care. The latter is likely to be the only option if you are going abroad. If they are to be put into someone's care, they should, if possible, be left in their own familiar cage. While being transported, the guinea-pigs should be protected from draughts and, as far as possible, prevented from becoming overexcited, so loosely cover the cage with a blanket or cloth. At the same time, make sure that they are receiving adequate ventilation.

Opposite and below: This is how to hold a guinea-pig securely and comfortably with both hands.

If you are only travelling a short distance, the guinea-pigs can be carried in a strong, firm **cardboard box** with plenty of air-holes. It is very important to cover the floor of the box with sawdust, wood shavings or a thick layer of tissue. Cover this with plenty of hay.

More substantial **carrying containers** are far better and absolutely essential when travelling greater distances. Nowadays, you can obtain such containers, made of transparent plastic and equipped with a well-ventilated cover and carrying grips. Again, the layer of wood shavings or tissue is very important to

Above and opposite:
'Can I come for a
ride too?'

*A practical plastic
carrying container with
a ventilated cover.*

ensure the guinea-pigs remain dry. Hay gives them something
to nibble on and calms them down. Also, the guinea-pigs can
hide in the hay.

The transparent wall of the container will enable you to keep an
eye on the animals during the journey. Tame guinea-pigs that are
used to this method of transport will be able to look out of the
transparent wall. However, if you are transporting very shy
animals, dark conditions are often preferable.

The carrying containers of guinea-pigs that are usually kept in
warm surroundings should be covered with blankets or other
fabrics when they are being transported during the colder months
of the year. Again, make sure that the guinea-pigs have plenty of
fresh air while being transported.

Breeding

Pregnancy and birth

Rabbits are well known for their speed of reproduction. A similar
state of affairs exists in guinea-pigs and they mature very early.
Females are sexually mature as early as 28 days after birth – in
exceptional cases at 20 days of age – and males can reproduce at
about 60–75 days after birth.

Young guinea-pigs should be separated according to sex very early if you do not want any more guinea-pig offspring to be produced. They will take a little longer to be mature enough for breeding purposes.

Female guinea-pigs should not be used for breeding purposes until they are at least 4–5 months old, preferably 6 months old, and males when they are 6–7 months old. However, females should be allowed to breed before the age of 9 months because, after this time, the pelvic bones become fused. The risk of a mother experiencing difficulties in giving birth are therefore greatly increased because it is difficult for the young to pass through the birth canal as they are born.

This is the best way to sex guinea-pigs. Left: A male (white) with a clearly visible penis. Right: A female (brown).

After a **gestation period** of 59–74 days, with an average of 68 days, usually one to six youngsters are born. Generally, there are only one or two babies in the first litter. Some guinea-pig families frequently produce four or five young but not, as a rule, until the second litter. Sextuplets are rare and litters of seven or eight youngsters are even rarer.

In a very few young animals, the gestation time tends to be closer to 74 days, but in most guinea-pigs it is closer to the 59 days mentioned above.

As early as 3–4 weeks after conception, your veterinarian may be able to detect the foetuses in the mother's belly. There are hardly any warning signals of an imminent birth in guinea-pigs, even though the female becomes quite rotund, particularly if the litter is going to be large.

Guinea-pigs are always born head first.

The mother takes up a hunched position when giving **birth**, and adopts this same position when suckling her young. As soon as the new-born baby has emerged, the mother will pull it towards her while it is still covered in membranes, break the membranes open and eat them. She will then lick her baby dry. In the case of multiple births, the next baby will emerge very quickly. As long as the guinea-pig mother does not appear to be in distress, you should not interfere.

Birth often takes place under cover of darkness, with the young being found in the quarters in the morning. Keep a close watch on the female's appetite at first. If this decreases, it could be indicative of **pregnancy toxaemia**. If this is the case, she will soon start to have severe convulsions and, without immediate veterinary treatment, in the hope of alleviating these symptoms, death will inevitably follow.

The first days of life

Guinea-pigs are able to see and hear immediately after birth and are also born with a fully developed coat of fur. Their eyes begin to open as early as 2 weeks before they are born. The milk teeth

The mother crouches to nurse her young.

also break through between the 43rd and the 48th day of gestation and, by the 55th day, have already been reabsorbed. At birth, all the permanent teeth are already present and only the back molars have still to break through the gum line.

The weights of new-born guinea-pigs may differ considerably, but usually lie between 45 and 110 g (1$^{1}/_{2}$ and 4 oz). Exceptional weights of up to 140 g (5 oz) have been recorded. Young animals born singly are, as a rule, heavier than those from multiple births. A single-birth individual weighing 100 g (3$^{1}/_{2}$ oz) is not a rarity. On the other hand, young animals from large litters, as a rule, only weigh about 50–80 g (1$^{3}/_{4}$ –2$^{7}/_{8}$ oz).

Their weight remains constant during the first few days after birth and may even drop by a few

grams. After that, the youngsters, if they are healthy, will gain weight steadily, at a rate of about 3–4 g (less than 1/8 oz) daily, up to the age of 6–8 weeks.

Baby guinea-pigs begin to run about as early as a few hours after their birth. The babies of litters of five, six or more have the best opportunities for rapid growth if other mother guinea-pigs are present in the cage. The young of the various different litters will then suckle from several different mothers, provided that there is no great age difference between the young. The mother has two teats situated in the area of the groin.

Young guinea-pigs begin to take solid food even during the first few days of their lives. For their well-being, and to ensure that they have an adequate supply of Vitamin B complex and Vitamin K, it is vital that they eat the faeces of the mother.

Young guinea-pigs with a birth weight of less than 40 g (1 1/2 oz) often do not survive, even if they are fed continually on milk from another source, with a pipette. It is difficult to artificially nurse and rear normal-weight young during the first few days of their lives because they are dependent to a considerable degree on their mother's milk. Coffee-creamer, which largely resembles guinea-pig milk in composition, especially in its fat and protein content, can be warmed to body heat and used as a substitute.

Young guinea-pigs can be separated from their mothers at the age of 3–4 weeks without any problems.

The well-known fertility of guinea-pigs is due not only to their very early maturity but also to the mother becoming fertile again within $1^{3}/_{4}$–13 hours of the birth, at which time she can success-fully conceive again. A simple calculation will reveal that, during the space of a year, a single pair of guinea-pigs is capable of producing 100 offspring, although, obviously, this is not to be recommended!

Age and weight of guinea-pigs

After about 13–17 days, the birth weight of the young guinea-pigs is doubled. At the age of 4–8 weeks, guinea-pigs weigh between 250 and 400 g ($8^{3}/_{4}$–14 oz), although the widely varying birth weight of individual animals is often reflected up to several weeks after their birth.

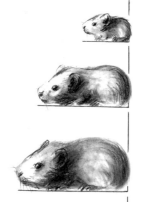

Guinea-pigs continue to grow up to the age of 15 months, even though the speed of growth slows down considerably with increasing age. In the end, males will weigh between 1,000 and 1,800 g (35 and $63^{1}/_{2}$ oz) and females between 700 and 1,000 g ($24^{1}/_{2}$ and 35 oz). Any weights greater than this will usually be due to excessive fat deposits.

Guinea-pigs generally live to an age of 5–8 years, although a few may live for 10 years or longer. A guinea-pig can usually be classified as 'old' at about 6 years of age, and definitely when it is aged about 7 years.

An ageing guinea-pig often begins to lose body mass because it can no longer utilize its food properly. In addition to sufficient hay and greenfood, it will then require increased amounts of nutri-ent-rich foods, e.g. carrots, and a higher proportion of concen-trates, such as pellets, plus an additional multi-vitamin preparation if needed. You should also ensure that there are sufficient amounts of minerals and trace elements in its diet.

A comparison of age and body size. From top to bottom: New-born, about 9.5 cm (less than 4 in); 5 weeks old, about 19 cm (under 8 in); 4 months old, about 23 cm (9 in); adult, about 27 cm (11 in).

Particular consideration should be given to an adequate supply of Vitamin C. This should amount to at least 30 mg/kg body weight per animal daily. Older guinea-pigs, which may have problems gnawing and therefore eat less hard food, often like to eat diced cucumber or melon.

A coat which is no longer shiny or which is becoming sparse is also an indication of age-related problems.

Old guinea-pigs, which generally may have a weakened immune system, can become susceptible to skin complaints. As a result, fungal diseases, as well as mites and other ectoparasites, will become more easily established than in younger guinea-pigs.

A guinea-pig investigates some pieces of birch branch.

The senses of guinea-pigs

Hearing
The inner ear of the guinea-pig is longer and more closely coiled than that of mice and rats, and even of human beings. As a result, the guinea-pig has exceptionally good hearing. It can hear sound frequencies up to 33,000 Hz whereas human beings can only perceive sound frequencies up to 20,000 Hz (when young) or 15,000 Hz (when adult).

Guinea-pigs rely heavily on their sense of smell.

Smell
The sense of smell in guinea-pigs is related mainly to contact with each other and to sexual behaviour.

Urine plays an important role as a scent-marker. Males that are ready to mate will spray their urine. Females that are not ready to mate will demonstrate their unwillingness by producing a certain scent, as well as by displaying rejective behaviour.

Guinea-pigs from a particular social group will recognize each other by their scent. This applies even when a lost youngster is reintroduced to the group.

It should be pointed out here that this group-connected recognition will be lost, even in adults, if they are separated from the group for several days. The marking of territory with secretions, and also with urine, explains why guinea-pigs feel comfortable in their usual surroundings and often become increasingly upset and insecure in unfamiliar surroundings. This is indicated by their timid behaviour.

Typical contact between two guinea-pigs through sniffing.

In comparison with human beings, guinea-pigs possess a much more highly developed sense of smell, up to 100 times more sensitive. They can often pick up scents that a human being would never notice and become excited by them in various different ways.

This sense of smell plays an important role when consuming food and can even be used to differentiate between edible and non-edible foods. The same applies to their recognition of individual human beings.

Sight

Because of the position of their eyes, guinea-pigs can see what is in front of them, as well as to the side, without having to move their head. In the wild, this relatively wide angle of vision is particularly important for protecting themselves from natural enemies. At the very least, guinea-pigs can also distinguish between the primary colours: red, yellow, blue and green. This plays an important part in feeding.

Touch

By means of the sensory hairs around the mouth and nose, guinea-pigs can determine, even in the dark, whether they will be able to pass through a hole or opening. They can also sense objects that constitute obstacles.

Opposite: Guinea-pigs rapidly become tame and really like being stroked.

Taste

If a guinea-pig is unable to make a definite distinction or decision on an individual piece of food using its highly developed sense of

38

Guinea-pigs are used to living and playing together in small groups.

smell, it will rely on its sense of taste. Both instinctive reactions in guinea pigs and previous experience then play a part, for example, in distinguishing between wholesome food they can eat and bad food.

Guinea-pigs are said to prefer sweet to sour foods, although bitter-tasting substances do not seem to bother them. However, individual guinea-pigs show definite differences in taste which are demonstrated by the different types of foods which they each prefer.

Sounds and communication

Guinea-pigs have a large repertoire of sounds.

Compared with other rodents, such as hamsters and mice, guinea-pigs produce quite a varied repertoire of sounds which are audible to our ears.

This ranges from a kind of murmuring, as an expression of satisfaction; cooing, on making contact with each other or for initiating mating behaviour – usually mainly expressed by males; to chattering of the teeth as a definite warning of an

40

imminent dispute between adult males about matters of hierarchy.

Young guinea-pigs emit high-pitched squeaking sounds that stimulate the mother or, in a group situation, another female, to pay attention to the youngsters. Guinea-pig mothers tend to react less and less to these cries for help as the youngsters become older, i.e. from about 14 days onwards, thereby forcing the young guinea-pigs to become independent.

Adult guinea-pigs also squeak, in a manner that is obviously a sign of fear, even to human beings. If a guinea-pig is rejected by a member of its group, the entire group will often flee in single file along a wall or projection. This is because, in the wild, this kind of feature provides relatively more protection, particularly from predatory birds, than dashing out into the open.

Guinea-pigs prefer a lofty vantage point.

Situations do arise in which a guinea-pig will be subject to a kind of paralysis through sheer fright. Again this type of behaviour has a protective role because it can deter an attack.

Their group-typical scent will often cause guinea-pigs to march along in single file.

If you inadvertently handle a guinea-pig clumsily, so that you hurt it, it will emit a series of characteristic shrill squeals.

Can your guinea-pigs learn?

Guinea-pigs are quite capable of learning to respond to their names, and to certain calls or whistles. It is important that you first allow the guinea-pigs to become accustomed to you. Have plenty of patience and let these naturally reticent creatures become trusting and lose their shyness. Thoughtless, quick movements, loud noises, etc. can easily wipe out all the good progress made during several days of effort.

A guinea-pig that is kept as a solitary pet should be regularly given plenty of attention or else its natural behavioural repertoire will gradually be lost, at least partially. You should always remember that guinea-pigs are not naturally solitary animals but are used to living in groups.

Will your guinea-pigs get on with other pets?

Some guinea-pigs will not run away from a dog, provided that they are accustomed to it and the dog behaves appropriately.

Right, below and opposite: *Guinea-pigs are not solitary animals and are very sociable – as these photographs of them climbing and playing together show. As can be seen, even a dwarf rabbit will be wecomed.*

However, you should never leave a dog alone with a guinea-pig as it could kill your pet.

Cats in particular always tend to look upon guinea-pigs as prey. A cat can upset them by jumping against the side of the cage and it may even try to push a paw through the bars or wire mesh, if they are widely spaced, to try and claw the guinea-pigs.

As a rule, it is not advisable to keep guinea-pigs together with other animals, even birds, particularly parrots and even smaller species such as budgerigars. There is also little sense in keeping them with other rodents, e.g. mice, rats, golden or dwarf hamsters, chinchillas or squirrels. Guinea-pigs, generally, never become aggressive but they can suffer from contact with other species.

Rabbits are the exception and the two species can live quite harmoniously together. There are usually no problems if an adult guinea-pig is kept with an appropriately sized dwarf rabbit or

possibly even a larger one. Guinea-pigs are quite happy sharing meals with rabbits. The animals may also rest or sleep closely cuddled up to each other and will groom each other's fur. Some guinea-pigs will enthusiastically sit on the neck or back of their rabbit companions.

The sick guinea-pig

The differences between sick and healthy guinea-pigs have already been described on p.6–9. Here are some notes on recognizing the most common diseases.

Parasites

Worms, **fleas** and **lice** are seldom a problem in guinea-pigs. **Mites**, however, occur rather more often and are generally spread by contact between individuals and contaminated surroundings, including bedding. **Mange** can be caused by various types of mites. Powders may help but the best option today is an injection of a suitable ivermectin preparation from the veterinarian. This may need to be repeated and the hutch will need to be cleaned thoroughly with a safe disinfectant. Lice may affect guinea-pigs occasionally. Treatment is similar to that for infestation with mites.

Lice favour the areas around the eyes and ears of guinea-pigs.

43

Tick infestations are rarely encountered, except in rural areas, and will only occur if the guinea-pigs are allowed to run about in a garden or on a balcony shaded by branches of trees or bushes. They should be removed by a veterinarian.

Symptoms of common ailments

Fungal infections seem to be particularly common in guinea-pigs that have been given only concentrated food for a long period, i.e. a diet deficient in raw fibre. The first symptom is the fur around the head dropping out in round or oval patches. The veterinarian will have to initiate an appropriate course of treatment. The symptoms can sometimes be similar to those of a mite infestation and tests may be needed to distinguish between them.

Diarrhoea is a symptom of inflammation of the stomach or intestines, usually connected with harmful substances in the food. The problem can often be resolved by the use of medicinal charcoal. If it persists for more than a day or so, you should definitely consult a veterinarian.

The importance of guinea-pigs in their countries of origin.

Bloating and **indigestion**, caused by the formation of gas in the hugely convoluted large intestine, may restrict the respiration, interfere with the action of the heart, and finally lead to death through suffocation and/or heart failure. Severe cases should be seen by a veterinarian as soon as possible.

Constipation may be due to an inadequate supply of fluid, e.g. the result of too much dry food in the diet or an inadequate supply of drinking water. Early on, the symptoms can be alleviated by giving plenty of drinking water and more moist, juicy foods. If this is unsuccessful, consult a veterinarian.

Respiratory illnesses can be caused by a bacterial or viral infection. They are most likely to arise if the guinea-pig has become chilled. The chance of infection is immediately increased in guinea-pigs suffering from a lack of Vitamin C, when the respiratory tract becomes very susceptible to the viruses and bacteria that may cause **pneumonia**.

Scurf, hair loss and even **cracking of the skin** may also all be linked with a **Vitamin C deficiency**.

Bite wounds, which may be quite extensive after a battle between adult guinea-pigs, should preferably be treated with a suitable antiseptic if necessary. This also applies to other types of wounds.

The relatives and ancestors of guinea-pigs

All representatives of the guinea-pig subfamily (Caviinae Murray, 1866) are exclusively South American in origin. The wild guinea-pig (*Cavia aperea*), also referred to as the aperea, is widely distributed throughout South America.

There is some dispute over the taxonomy of these rodents but, as a result of the subfamily's very wide distribution, nine sub-species, or geographical races, are generally recognized. One of them, *Cavia aperea tschudii*, lives along both sides of the Andes range. It is dark cinnamon-grey, with a reddish yellow or grey back, a reddish yellow to whitish belly and usually a light-coloured spot in the area of the throat. The longer, relatively dark guard hairs create a shading of colours reminiscent of that found on the backs of wild rabbits. These guard hairs can be so dark that the back may appear almost black.

Unlike golden hamsters, guinea-pigs are active by day.

All domestic guinea-pigs are descended from this subspecies. Their domestication may have begun even before the Inca period, during which time they were first used as sacrificial animals and then as a supply of meat. A poor Inca would sacrifice a guinea-pig whereas a rich one would sacrifice a llama.

From discoveries of mummified guinea-pigs, we know that, even in those days, guinea-pig fur came in a variety of colours. Only black fur, either as a single colour or as an element of patching, was never recorded from any of the animals found. Because black was the colour of malevolent spirits or evil, it is thought that black guinea-pigs may have been killed immediately at birth.

Even nowadays, domestic guinea-pigs are a valuable source of meat among the indigenous South Americans of the High Andes. For this purpose, in Peru, Colombia, Ecuador and Bolivia, particu-larly large guinea-pigs are bred weighing up to 2,500 g (5½ lb) or more. In Peru, an estimated 67 million guinea-pigs are kept and provide about 17,000 tonnes (16,728 tons) of meat each year.

In South America, many customs and beliefs connected with guinea-pigs and dating from the Inca period still exist to this day, e.g., the superstition that guinea-pigs attract diseases, a belief that existed even in Europe in past times.

The first guinea-pigs arrived in Spain and Portugal very soon after the discovery of the New World in 1492 and, from there, spread to the UK and the Netherlands. They were quite rare to begin with and appropriately expensive. One guinea-pig was

worth a whole guinea (£1.05 sterling), which was a lot of money in those days. It is therefore believed that the name 'guinea-pig' originated from that period and was given to the little creature whose voice and body build resembled that of a small pig.

The domestic guinea-pig was given a Latin name, *Cavia porcellus*, by Linnaeus as long ago as 1758. Of course, any domesticated animal should only receive a scientific designation that reflects its wild origins so nowadays the domestic guinea-pig is known as *Cavia aperea tschudii* forma *porcellus*. Alternatively, it could also be referred to as *Cavia aperea tschudii* forma *domestica*.

To conclude, here are some of the names given to the little creature in other languages: French – *cochon d'Inde* or *cobaye*; German – *Meerschweinchen*; Spanish – *cobayo*; Russian – *morskaya swinya*. English-speakers also refer to the guinea-pig as 'cavy' or 'cui', the first name resembles the Latin name, while the second is derived from the Quechua Indian words *cui* and *cuy*, names that mimic the sounds which the animal makes.

Index

Picture sources
All photographs are by Regina Kuhn except those on page 28 which are by Dietrich Altmann. Black-and-white illustrations are by Siegfried Lokau, as specified by the author.

Acknowledgements
The animals photographed for this book were kindly supplied by Zoo-Kolle, of Stuttgart and Zoo-Utke, of Esslingen.

A BLANDFORD BOOK

First published in the UK 1997 by Blandford
A Cassell imprint
Cassell plc Wellington House 125 Strand London WC2R 0BB

Text copyright © 1997 Cassell plc
Translated by Astrid Mick
Originally published as *Meerschweinchen* by Dietrich Altmann
World copyright © Eugen Ulmer GmbH & Co., Stuttgart, Germany

Distributed in the United States by
Sterling Publishing Co., Inc.,387 Park Avenue South, New York, NY 10016-8810

A Cataloguing-in-Publication Data entry for this title is available from the British Library

ISBN 0-7137-2681-4

Printed and bound in Spain